Food

BERYL AUSTONI • ALAN GOODIER

SERIES EDITORS: PETER BRANSON • JONATHAN RENAUDON-SMITH

CAMBRIDGE
UNIVERSITY PRESS

Published by the Press Syndicate of the University of Cambridge
The Pitt Building, Trumpington Street, Cambridge CB2 1RP
40 West 20th Street, New York, NY 10011-4211, USA
10 Stamford Road, Oakleigh, Melbourne 3166, Australia

First published 1996

Produced by Gecko Limited, Bicester, Oxon

Printed in Great Britain at the University Press, Cambridge

A catalogue record for this book is available from the British Library

ISBN 0 521 49874 0

Cover – Food pyramid.

Cover design by Ralf Zeigermann

Acknowledgements
The authors and publisher would like to thank the following
for their help during the preparation of this book.
Riccardo Austoni, Brian Elliott and all the staff at Cryovac;
Hinchingbrooke School;
Louise Jones, Lisa McGowan and all the staff at Pret A
Manger;
Colin Munday and all the staff at Weetabix Limited,
Kettering;
Keith Piper;
Technology Teaching Systems.
Diagrams on pages 43 and 44 adapted from APME
publication *Plastics packaging – friend or enemy?*

The publisher would like to thank the following for
permission to reproduce copyright photographs.
Art Directors' Photo Library 19;
G. Buss/Telegraph Colour Library cover;
Cryovac 39 tl, 48;
Robert Opie Collection 42;
Graham Portlock 6, 8–9, 24, 26, 27, 29, 36–37, 38, 39br,
41br, 46;
J. Sainsbury plc 41tr;
The Rt Hon Earl of Sandwich for permission to
photograph 26;
Weetabix Limited 7, 11, 12, 13.

Contents

Product development

DESIGN BRIEF

SPECIFICATION and
QUALITY INDICATORS

CONCEPTUAL DESIGN

PRESENTATION OF IDEAS
and EVALUATION

FINAL SPECIFICATION

DESIGN for
MARKETABLE PRODUCTION

PRODUCTION PLAN
and SCHEDULE

PRODUCTION

LAUNCH / MARKETING

Breakfast

The traditional English breakfast of bacon, eggs, sausage, fried bread and a selection of regional foods has largely disappeared from our homes. This is due to our changing lifestyles and the nutrition advice from dietitians.

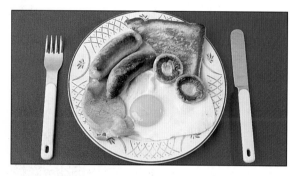

▲ *Traditional English breakfast.*

Find out what the members of your group have for breakfast.

Now that more women go out to work, the early morning is a busy time in families, and there is no time for a cooked breakfast. Also, since the 1970s nutrition experts have advised that we should reduce the amounts of fat, sugar and salt that we eat and increase our intake of fibre. This has made the fatty, traditional breakfast less popular. The COMA (Committee on Medical Aspects) report recommended that the amount of energy we obtain from our daily intake of fat be reduced to below 35% if we are to reduce the heart disease rate.

Dietary fibre is present in fruit and vegetables and also in bread, pasta and cereal products. Doctors agree that fibre reduces constipation and may help to prevent some diseases, particularly cancers of the colon.

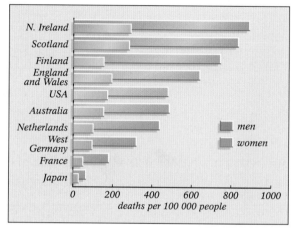

▲ *Death rates from coronary heart disease in 55–64 year olds.*

Cereals have become the main food eaten at breakfast, because they are quick and easy to prepare and eat, they are filling and they can contribute to a healthy diet. There is a large range of cereals available to cater for all tastes and ages: a supermarket may stock as many as 150 types of cereal. This was not the case in the 1950s, when relatively few varieties were sold. A number of these cereals were only sold in health-food shops, which were then less widespread and catered for a minority of people.

Survey your local supermarket and count the number of breakfast cereals available. Categorise them into mainstream, health-conscious and children's varieties.
Interview 50 people of various ages to find out the most popular cereals within these age groups:
5–11   12–18   19–30   31–45   45+
Find out the cereal they usually eat and why they choose that variety. You could use a database to record the information.

Every morning, millions of people around the world will eat a breakfast cereal. Weetabix started producing its famous wholewheat cereal biscuits in the early 1930s, and they are still popular. When it started, the company only sold to local shops. As the product gained in popularity, a sales force had to be employed so that Weetabix could be sold to the whole country.

During the Second World War (1939–1945), problems with the availability of raw materials meant that Weetabix was only available in the Midlands and the North East of England. The wartime diet was very healthy, primarily because it included rationing of meat and fats. Rationing also provided a fair method of distributing food that was in short supply, because people of the same age were each allowed the same amount of food. Bread and vegetables were not rationed, and so everyone had a plentiful and healthy supply of fibre.

▲ *Weetabix product range.*

Research the contents of a 1940s diet in Britain. Perhaps you could interview older members of your family or people you know to find out what they remember.

After the War, Weetabix expanded rapidly to provide a serious challenge to its two major competitors from the USA. The company developed and expanded on its site near Kettering in Northamptonshire. By 1970, the company had grown from a small family business to become the largest British-owned breakfast-cereal manufacturer. The production lines have become increasingly automated, and in 1995 the Kettering factory could produce more than 70 million biscuits each week (that's about 100 every second!). The company also makes Alpen on this site, and other breakfast cereals at its factories in nearby Corby.

Alpen was introduced in 1971, and was developed from a Swiss product range called 'muesli', which was sold here, mainly in health-food shops, from the 1960s. Alpen muesli is still a brand-leader, in spite of fierce competition from other manufacturers and supermarket **'own-label'** products.

Weetabix have added other products to their range, so that there is something to appeal to everyone who eats cereal for breakfast. The company now produces cereals in Canada and the USA, where the idea of breakfast cereals was started.

Although cereals are usually eaten at breakfast, they are also eaten at other times of the day. They are an important part of our daily diet.

You should now understand:
- **the changes in diet that have occurred since the 1940s,**
- **the trends in people's eating habits at breakfast,**
- **the importance of breakfast in a healthy diet.**

You will now be able to complete the task below, which may form part or all of your coursework.

- Ask four people, one from each of the following age ranges:

  7–11   12–18   25–40   60+

  to write down all they eat in one day.
- Use the information to analyse the diets to find out if they are healthy. (You may be able to use a computer program for the analysis, for example a food database or information on a CD-ROM.)
- Compare the amount of fat and fibre they eat with the dietary recommendations for their age group.
- Produce a diet sheet for one of the people, showing them how to improve their diet.
- For each person, design and make a healthy breakfast that supplies about one third of their daily needs.

Developing new products

All manufacturers need to develop and update their products to take account of the needs of consumers, the demands of the market and the products developed by other manufacturers. Food manufacturers have to update and modify their products in the same way as a car maker, for example, to enable them to keep one step ahead of the opposition by selling more.

Weetabix research constantly to help them retain their position as brand leader. They have to develop new products to assist them in expanding their sales. Prior to introducing Weetos, a new cereal, to their product range, Weetabix had to consider the costs involved in setting up a new production line, as new machinery is very expensive.

0 – 1 month	identifying a market – market research and analysis
1 – 3 months	developing a product specification – what it will look and taste like
3 – 6 months	producing concept samples – samples of new products which might fit the specification
6 – 9 months	prototype samples
9 – 12 months	factory trials

▲ *Sketch of time-line start.*

Discuss the considerations that a company must make before they decide to develop a new product. For example, what is the target market? (An answer to this might be 'children'.) What will any new equipment cost? Put the considerations in order of priority, and work out a time-line leading up to the launch date.

Market research plays an important part in the working of any company. The opinions of consumers are researched and recorded during the development and piloting stages of a new product. Companies need to know what customers want so that a new product will be a financial success. Manufacturers need to be confident that the product will be popular before they develop the production line, buy the raw materials and market the product. Before the launch of the Weetos range, Weetabix needed to know more about their potential customers. They surveyed specific age ranges within the target age group. The survey used carefully constructed questions to determine people's requirements as precisely as possible.

Carry out a survey to find out what type of new breakfast cereal could be a success. Choose a target age group before you write the survey. Interview at least 30 people and use a database to record the results. Write a specification for this new product, so that it could be presented to a cereal manufacturer.

More about ... questionnaires page 50.

The development of new products may be prompted by a new idea. In this case the company is *pushing* the market: they are in charge of the development and leading the field. If the development is in response to a new product from a rival company, then the market is *pulling* the company into action to defend their share of the market. This pulling action may also be instigated by other factors, such as the health lobby – doctors and those people who research the national diet.

Competition is very fierce because the breakfast cereal market is so large. In order to survive as a profitable company, Weetabix invest in research and development. They keep their developments, recipes and processes secret and limit the access of visitors in the factory. This is common and accepted practice in all industries, and it is the reason why we cannot provide a recipe and a method for making Weetabix.

The development of new machinery and processing methods can also pull the market into the development of new products. Sometimes new products or processes are discovered during the testing stages of other new products or equipment. A well documented example of this is the discovery of the glue for self-sticking removable notes, when a well known glue manufacturing company developed a new adhesive and the formulation went wrong.

The introduction of new packaging and preservation methods play an important role in food product development, especially for those products that have a short **shelf-life**. Food must remain safe to eat and be in the best possible condition, up to and a little beyond the **'Best Before' date**. Manufacturers must test the shelf-life of

a new product at the development stage, so that they can determine a 'Best Before' date. If the product has a short shelf-life relative to competing products, it will probably not be successful.

Tasting and testing

In order to develop new products or recipes, and to monitor the quality of existing lines, Weetabix conduct many laboratory and sensory analysis tests.

The tests conducted in the laboratory usually examine the quality of raw materials, to discover the correct processes for manufacturing and to identify any problems with production. The Quality Audit team take samples from the production line at various times during the day, and these samples are checked for quality. For example, biscuits are tested for moisture, breakage, density and texture. These tests are particularly important during the development of a new product or recipe, so that a standard is established and a specification can be written.

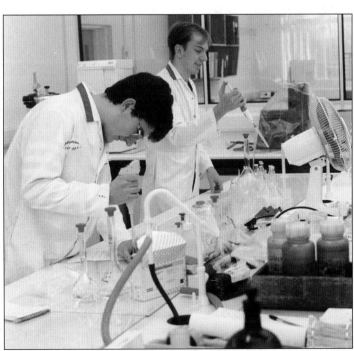

The laboratory at Weetabix. ▶

▲ *Testing samples from each product line.*

• Description

What does the product taste like? How do changes in processing, recipe, packaging and storage conditions affect its sensory characteristics?

At Weetabix, sensory analysis is used to check on various aspects of development and production.

The Factory Manager, Plant Managers, Shift Managers, Supervisors and Quality Auditors meet at predetermined regular intervals to examine samples from each production line. This is a forum to discuss the production situation in each plant, and it helps to ensure that Weetabix produce consistently high-quality products. Quality Audit, also known as **quality control**, is a vital part of all manufacturing processes, which ensures that products meet set specifications consistently.

Sensory analysis tests are used in the development of new products and recipes. These measure the characteristics of a product as perceived by our senses: sight, sound, smell, taste and touch.

Sensory analysis

• Preference/liking

How much does a person like a product? Which attributes do they like? Is the product as good as the competition? Is it the preferred product?

• Discrimination

Can someone detect a difference between one product and another? How many people would detect this difference? Is one sample the same as another?

Shelf-life

The shelf-life is the time it takes for the product to become unacceptable to the consumer. Analysis shows how the sensory qualities change with time and how long it takes for these changes to make the product unacceptable. The results determine the shelf-life.

> Conduct a tasting test of a product that has a shelf-life of about two months, for example crisps. Check a fresh sample and compare it to ones that have been stored, including one which has reached its 'Best Before' date, to find out if you can detect any deterioration in the product.

 Do not eat food which has been opened previously in the shop or stored beyond the 'Best Before' date.

Product matching

This is used to compare the characteristics of one product to those of another. The testing method is based on descriptive tests. For example, a target product made in a pilot plant may be compared with a sample from the production line. (The target product is the one which is thought to be ideal.) Does the sample match the target product? If the sample differs, how does it differ and how can it be made more like the target product?

Product mapping

This is used to identify the position of a product with respect to those of the competitors. Descriptive tests are used. For example, how do the company's Weeta Flakes compare with other brands? What are the sensory differences among the products? What are the attributes of those liked most and least?

Product reformulation and product development

Product prototypes can be compared against one another. The testing methods used are discrimination, description and preference/liking. This gives information regarding changes to make the product more like the target. The effects of recipe or processing changes on the sensory characteristics of every product can also be shown. In addition, information that shows which attributes are liked or disliked and which product is preferred can be judged. What is the effect of altering the ingredients or the processing? Which product is preferred?

- Choose a simple recipe for small cakes or biscuits and make a small batch.
- Make changes to the recipe and produce a further batch for each change you make. (You could change the amount or type of flour, for example.)
- Test each batch produced to see which is preferred.

Taints

Taints are flavours or odours that should not be present in a product. If a product is found to be tainted, consumers may complain and the reputation of the company may suffer. Therefore, testers check carefully for taints. Discriminative and descriptive tests are used. Is there a detectable difference in flavour or odour from the target product? If there is, what is the flavour or odour? The number of testers who detect the odour or flavour is measured, to establish whether or not the taint is a serious problem (if only a small minority of the testers detect the taint, then it is not a serious problem).

Product acceptability

This is used to assess how much one sample is liked compared to others. Preference/liking tests are used. Which product is preferred? How much do you like the product? How much do you like or dislike the appearance, flavour and texture?

At Weetabix, subjective and objective tests are used for analysis. You can set up subjective tests easily in school and they can be used for all food products. Objective tests give more detailed information but the testers have to be trained.

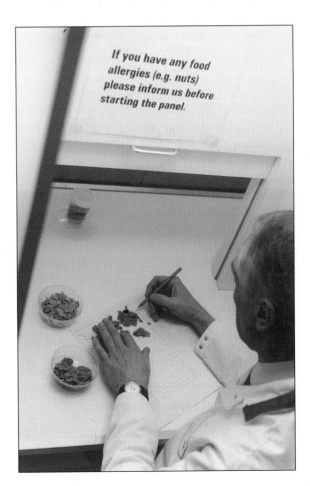

Consumer test in progress. ▶

Subjective tests

These are preference/liking tests and are often called 'consumer tests'. They provide information about which characteristics of a product are liked and which are disliked. In this type of testing there are no right or wrong answers. Untrained testers are used, and there should be over 30 testers for each sampling. Each tester is given two samples of the same product made to different specifications and an assessment form on which to record their opinions. A scale is used for each characteristic. Below is an example of a five-point scale:

What do you think of the colour of the samples?

```
I like it a lot
I quite like it
I neither like nor dislike it
I don't like it much
I don't like it at all
```

The results are collected and analysed to show the general pattern of opinion about the product. This gives some idea of how popular the product might be, and who would buy it.

Objective tests

These are used to give more detailed information about the product samples. They involve discriminating between samples and describing the properties of the product being tested – discriminative and descriptive tests. The tests are carried out by a small panel of trained testers.

Discrimination tests are conducted to find out whether any differences exist between samples. These objective tests are designed to show *actual* differences – the subjective tests may only show *imagined* differences.

A triangle test uses sets of two different samples, A and B. It is carried out by a panel of about 20 testers. The sets of samples are distributed so that half of the testers are given two of sample A and one of sample B; the other half are given one of sample A and two of sample B. The allocation of samples is made random, so that no tester knows how many of each sample they have. Each tester chooses the sample that is the 'odd one out'; if the samples are consistent then testers will detect clear differences between the product recipes.

A difference test is used to describe and measure the size of any differences between samples. The technique is called Quantitative Descriptive Analysis (QDA) and can be used to compare several samples at the same time. Twelve trained assessors are employed for this at Weetabix. For each new project, the assessors decide on a list of terms they will use to describe the samples. Each assessor must understand the meaning of each term, and special care must be taken to ensure that each assessor qualifies the terms in the same way. For example, if 'sweetness' is measured on a scale of 1 to 5, then each assessor must use the scale in the same way.

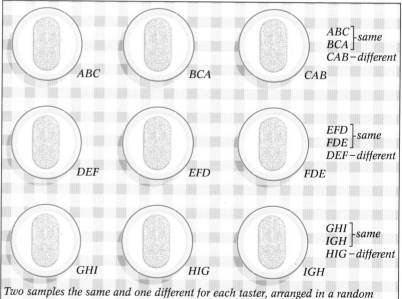

Two samples the same and one different for each taster, arranged in a random order that should be changed for each taster. The labelling must not give any indication of the samples.

▲ *Triangular taste testing.*

When the assessments are carried out, each assessor has their own separate booth to ensure that the analysis is unaffected by the other panellists. Each sample is assessed a number of times, usually three, to make any averages calculated more reliable. The results are analysed by a computer, and can be displayed on a star diagram.

When conducting sensory tests, food manufacturers have to make sure that all samples are uniform. For example, at Weetabix they control the amount of milk added to samples of cereal. Uniform lighting is used so that the product colours look the same. The assessors are provided with a weak lime juice to cleanse the mouth between samples, so that they can taste more accurately.

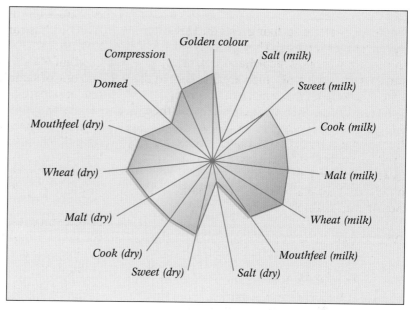

▲ A star diagram for Weetabix.

You should now understand:

- **products and applications with regard to breakfast products,**
- **how to conduct research,**
- **quality control,**
- **testing, particularly taste tests and product development tests.**

You will now be able to complete the task below, which may form part or all of your coursework.

Set up a series of tasting and testing panels to assess different manufacturers' versions of one type of breakfast cereal. Write up the results and make recommendations to manufacturers about their products.

Product design

Before designing a new product, a company conducts detailed product testing. It also conducts **market research** to find out the type of product required and at which area of the market it should be targeted. The marketing department then produces a Design Brief for the new product. The development team discuss this, and a **product specification** is written. This specification identifies the market, what the product will look and taste like, the ingredients required and the likely price. The specification must take into account what the plant (machinery) can do and the availability of raw materials. If the development will be expensive, perhaps because of a need for new machinery, then the specification must allow for the costs to be recouped from projected sales.

The research and development department prepares **concept samples**. When these have been tested, the brief and specification may need to be changed. From the 10–20 concept samples, 3–5 are selected for further development – these are the prototype products. During the development work, the prototypes are assessed by consumer and testing panels and modified as appropriate to achieve the optimum product.

For each prototype, the costs of both the machinery and the manufacturing process are calculated. These costs are then compared with the expected sales; if the company expects to recoup all the money it spends on a product, plus a certain amount of profit, then the product is **commercially viable**. The cost of manufacture must allow for the purchase of raw materials. For example, if the product contains exotic ingredients that need to be imported, then this will increase the cost of manufacture.

Labour, packaging and energy costs must be included. The **shelf-life** must also be taken into account, because it also influences costs (and hence profit margins). For example, a short shelf-life will increase wastage.

Once the best product has been decided upon, a production specification is written and the factory trials begin. Quantities of raw materials are set in this specification, so that suppliers can be informed.

The research and development department is involved in all stages of the product development, and will make adjustments as they are needed. The launch of the product is planned during this development period. A key part of the planning is the design of the advertising.

Whilst the factory trials are being conducted, an operating manual is written. The manual provides detailed instructions for each stage of the manufacturing process. Once the manual is complete, staff can be trained to carry out the manufacturing process, ready for when full-scale production starts.

The operating manual will conform to a standard called 'ISO 9000'. The International Standards Organisation (ISO) has drawn up this standard to assist companies in creating top-quality management systems. The original British Standard, BS 5750, has been redefined as BS.EN.ISO 9000 to conform to ISO.

A key function of the operating manual is to highlight **Hazard Analysis and Critical Control Points (HACCPs)**. These are the most important areas of the production line: hazard points, where safety precautions must be taken to protect the products from contamination, and critical control points, where key stages in the production are controlled to ensure that the product meets the specifications.

Weetabix regard their overall quality management as vital to the success of a product. The products are inspected at several stages of the manufacturing process, to ensure that standards are being met – this is **quality assurance**. At the end of the process, finished products are checked to ensure, for instance, that individual items are correctly wrapped and sealed – this is **quality control**.

You should now understand:
- **how a new food product is designed,**
- **that specifications are written for food products,**
- **quality assurance and quality control systems.**

You will now be able to complete the task below, which may form part or all of your coursework.

- You have been asked to develop a new breakfast product to add to the range of a cereal manufacturer.
- Decide on the target market and conduct research to establish what is needed.
- Think about what people around the world eat for breakfast – brainstorm your ideas.
- List some products you could make.
- Develop and taste-test products.
- If you are working in a team, pairs or individuals could concentrate on one aspect of the product development.
- Write a production specification. This should include what the product will look and taste like.
- Design the packaging and plan the marketing.
- Devise a manual to instruct a workforce about the manufacture of the product.

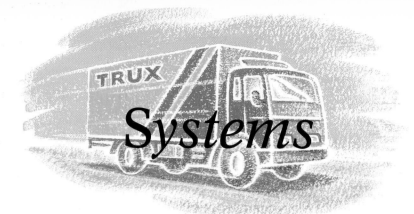

Systems

The word system is in common use today. For example, we talk about filing systems, weather systems and ticketing systems. You need to think about how you use the word system. A paper filing system may be a simple method of storing information. A computerised filing system may use sophisticated technology, both to control who can have access to particular information and to manipulate the information in lots of different ways.

Some systems may appear to be *organisational*, but actually rely on various technologies to operate. Managing the road traffic in a large city relies on the technology of traffic lights, cameras and traffic control centres to allow the authorities to operate a traffic management plan efficiently.

Defining systems

All four of the following points must apply if something is to be described as a system:

- the system is made up of parts or activities that do something,
- the parts or activities are connected together in an organised way,
- the parts or activities affect what is going through the system, so that it is changed when it leaves the system,
- the whole thing has been identified by humans as of interest.
  (Open University)

Hard or soft system?

A *soft system* involves an element of human decision-making. For example, the operators on the baking lines at Weetabix are alerted to changes in temperature (or other problems) by a combination of automated systems and control panels on the side of each oven. The operators can send information into the system by changing the controls, such as heater settings.

A *hard system*, by contrast, is self-regulating – human decision-making is excluded from the system and the controls are operated automatically. For example, thermostats can control the temperature inside an oven. A sensor detects the temperature and sends a control signal back to the heating element, switching the element off when the temperature rises above a set maximum and switching it on when the temperature falls below a set minimum. On page 23 you will see how to model this using an electronic systems kit.

Most mechanical and electrical systems can perform some or all of their actions automatically. Some systems operate automatically once they are installed and set up – for example, street lighting that switches on in dull weather or at night. Other systems have to be switched on, but then operate automatically. One example is a microwave oven, which has to be set and switched on before it will cook. The cooking proceeds automatically until the machine switches off and sounds a warning signal.

The manufacturing companies in this book use different production methods and systems to make their products. Weetabix have an organisational system that uses people, resources and equipment to produce quality products, which generate income for both the company and its workers. In order to operate

▲ *Food production system.*

efficiently, they have a supply system, which makes available the ingredients for their products when required. Computer control systems ensure that the products are always cooked to the same standard. Mechanical systems, such as conveyor belts, move the products through the production system and into the packing system.

Weetabix have developed sophisticated **quality assurance** procedures to check that their products meet the standards customers require. A distribution system ensures that all the products reach customers on time and in the best possible condition. Financial and economic systems ensure that invoices are issued and payments are made or received on time.

You use biological systems to process food within your body. When you eat the finished food product, your digestive system breaks it down into the parts your body requires to function – protein, vitamins and so on.

Think of a fresh-food product such as a fruit or a pint of milk. Make a list of the systems that are in place to bring the food into your local shop. Draw a flow-block diagram to represent the main parts of this process, for example:

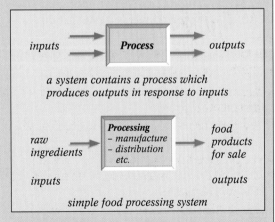

a system contains a process which produces outputs in response to inputs

simple food processing system

Look carefully at one part of the process and see if you can represent more clearly what is happening. (You will probably find that a flow-block diagram is still the best representation.) Remember to be clear about what is flowing in your diagram and what processes you are trying to describe.

The language of systems

A specialised language is used to describe systems. Flow-block diagrams give an outline of how the parts of a system link together. Individual blocks do not contain many words but do assume a lot of detail.

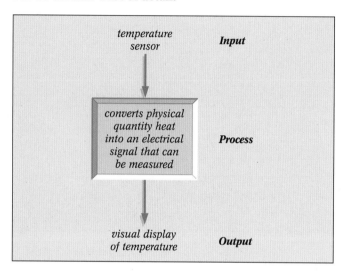

At the simplest level, a system can be represented as a box or a boundary, which contains a process that produces outputs in response to specific inputs. The simple flow-block diagram for a food production plant or fast-food outlet explains the basic principles.

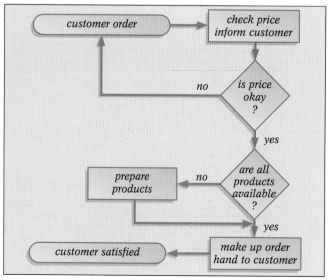

▲ *Block diagram for fast-food outlet.*

Manufacturing companies use flow-block diagrams to describe the sequence of events within processes and systems. Flow-block diagrams describe the relationship between inputs and outputs. This is important for design, because it provides greater flexibility at the planning stage of a new product or system. The process of product development is easier to outline without the distractions of having to consider the fine details. As the way you represent what is happening develops, more detail is provided. This *top-down* design is a more efficient use of time and human resources.

> For one or other of the following examples of processes, identify what the inputs and outputs might be.
> - Putting the chocolate on top of a biscuit.
> - Checking that a bottle has been filled to the correct level.
> - Making filter coffee (with a machine) in a catering outlet.
>
> Where do the food inputs come from? What other system may be involved in producing them?

In your product development and project work you need to make sure that you:

- get an accurate and detailed specification from your customer or target group,
- use a top-down or systems approach to design, to break the problem down into manageable sections.

At the detailed level of planning, when specific decisions have to be made, you will need to use a flow chart to illustrate the processes taking place. When producing a flow chart, you should use the standard set of symbols recommended by the British Standards Institution (BSI). (If you are not sure what these are, ask your information technology teachers – flow charts are an important aid in the process of programming computers.) There are three common symbols you should learn about first.

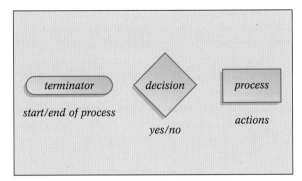

▲ Standard flow chart symbols.

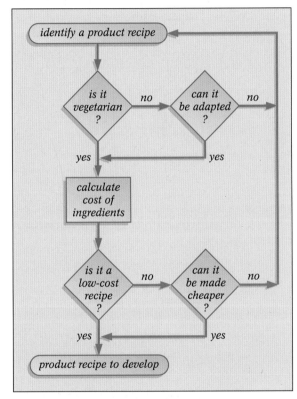

▲ Flow chart to produce a recipe for a low-cost vegetarian product.

Here is a simple flow chart for developing a food product.

Notice that there are two possible decisions you can make from any decision box. If the operation or process is not completed satisfactorily, a 'no' information signal is sent back to the system input until the operation or process is correct. This is an example of *feedback*.

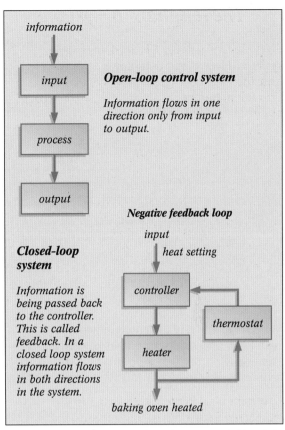

▲ Systems showing open-loop and closed-loop control.

Feedback information from an output to control an input is an essential part of most systems. It might be general information, such as customer feedback to a market researcher, or specific information, such as the drop in temperature in an oven.

Produce a flow chart showing the instructions followed and decisions made in boiling an egg.

Produce a flow-block diagram outlining a plan of action for producing a food product that you have made. It should identify the materials, equipment, tools, processes and quality assurance procedures you might use to **batch-produce** the product. Try to add more detail in one part of the diagram, in the form of flow charts.

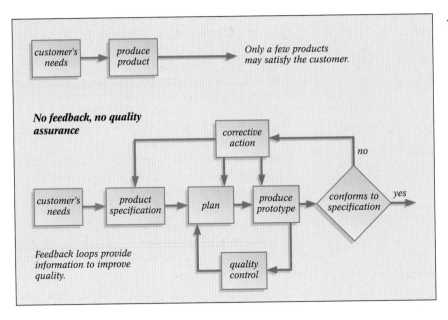

◀ Simple and complex quality assurance procedures.

When you mix and weigh ingredients for your own **'one-off' products**, you use feedback to check and control the amounts that you measure out.

> How would ingredients be measured at a company like Weetabix, where flow production is used?

Quality assurance procedures maintain, control and improve the quality of products, and services could not operate effectively without feedback of information.

Weetabix are constantly developing new products. These are tested through internal and external procedures, which are based on **market research** techniques such as the use of focus groups. A *focus group* consists of people specially selected to represent the target groups for a new product. Their opinions are used in product development. It takes time to respond to information gathered in this way. If the product is thought to be too sweet, it will take the company time to reformulate the ingredients and test the revised product. This time-delay is another key feature in some systems. It is known as *lag* and it exists in any closed-loop system. (Closed-loop systems involve the use of feedback.)

Investigating control systems

Any piece of electrical or mechanical equipment requires a control system to operate. It might be a simple on/off switch or a more sophisticated control system.

> Consider the operation of:
> - halogen hobs,
> - microwave ovens,
> - slow cookers.
>
> Produce a simple flow-block diagram for each cooking device to describe the main features of how it works.

Temperature control

Control of temperature is very important in the mass production of food. The baking ovens at Weetabix have temperature sensors built in to them to monitor and measure temperature. Control systems may also make use of *transducers*. Transducers are devices that transfer energy from one system to another. Many transducers also transform the energy, for example a temperature transducer transforms heat energy into electrical energy. They are often used to link systems to the outside world. There are two types of transducers – input and output. For example, a microphone is an input transducer and a loudspeaker is an output transducer.

> Consider how an electronic temperature probe works. It measures a physical quantity, temperature, and produces an electronic signal. This signal is measured and then displayed, usually as a visual display. Draw a flow-block diagram to illustrate this system. Label the input and output transducers.

A temperature sensor

Try setting up the temperature sensor circuit shown, using an electronic systems kit. The temperature sensor will monitor the temperature of the room you are in. It will sense changes in room temperature and the meter will show the changing electrical signal. The bulb should light when the temperature increases. Can you make the bulb light when the temperature falls?

You need to be able to set the temperature precisely for cooking and storage. For instance, the temperature of a chill cabinet should not rise above 4 °C. Ovens and cookers must work within a specified temperature range that can be easily and accurately adjusted.

The temperature of the storage environment can be compared with a set temperature. If the storage temperature goes above (or below) the set temperature, a warning bulb lights up. A *comparator* is used to compare the two signals (one from the temperature sensor, the other from the control that adjusts the set temperature). The comparator produces a signal (a response) that controls the bulb (the output transducer).

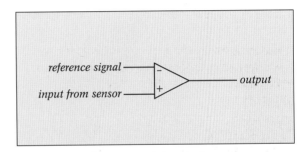

▲ *A comparator compares the actual output of a system with the desired output. If there is a difference, the comparator changes to correct the output.*

A comparator can also be set up to convert an analogue signal into a digital signal. Analogue signals vary continuously in size, digital signals are either on or off. For example, a musical instrument produces an analogue signal – you can play an instrument at any volume, from very quiet to extremely loud. However, a bleeper produces a digital signal, which is either on or off – nothing in-between.

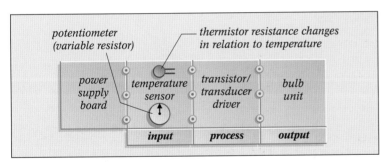

▲ *A temperature sensing system.*

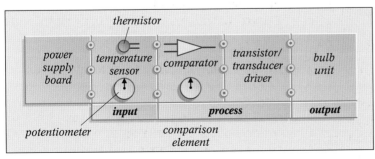

▲ *A temperature control system.*

A temperature probe, which you insert into a piece of meat to see if it is completely cooked, sends analogue signals related to the different temperature zones in the meat. However, you need to know what those temperatures are. A temperature probe usually has a digital display. The electronics inside the temperature probe process the analogue signals to produce the digital signal required for the visual display. The device that does this is called an analogue-to-digital (A/D) converter.

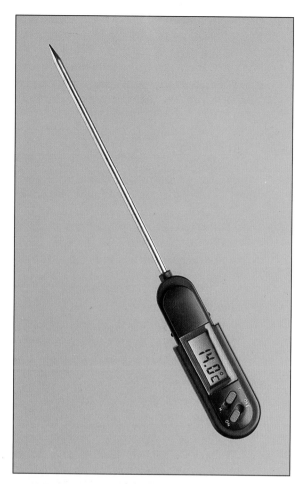

▲ *Microwave temperature probe.*

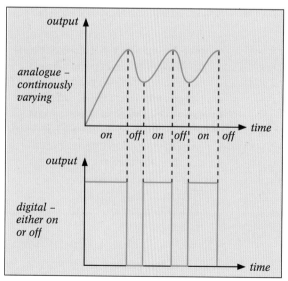

▲ *Analogue and digital signals.*

Control systems at Weetabix

Control systems are not always based on electronic transducers. At some points on the production line at Weetabix, the monitoring devices are mechanical, and these produce signals that are then fed into electronic or pneumatic control devices.

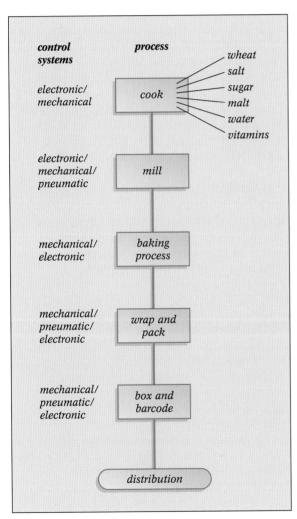

▲ *Simple production flow diagram.*

Instrumentation in industry

Instruments are integral parts of most control systems. They are used because:

- many processes are complicated and happen very quickly,
- they allow processes to run continuously,
- conditions can be monitored – the cooking of a Weetabix biscuit takes place over a range of temperatures rather than at one set temperature,
- they provide vital safety information,
- they produce signals that can be fed into computers or on-board microprocessors.

At Weetabix, these control systems are used extensively, to monitor and modify the food production processes. The use of control systems means that the production of a large number of similar products can be carried out consistently to the same quality level. Consistent quality is what consumers demand.

You should now understand:
- **how to represent systems,**
- **how systems are used in food production.**

You will now be able to complete the task below, which may form part or all of your coursework.

Design a process for producing a new type of potato crisp. Start out by drawing a flow-block diagram. Produce flow charts for those areas of the process where you need to see more detail. Remember to consider all the steps in the process, for example slicing the potatoes, baking them, adding flavourings, and so on. How important is the order in which these steps are carried out? What preparation is needed for the raw materials?

Selling sandwiches

The sandwich is said to have been invented by the fourth Earl of Sandwich in the eighteenth century. There are several versions of the story explaining why he asked for meat served between two slices of bread. One story says that, as Lord of the Admiralty, he was too busy to leave his work on naval documents for a full dinner, and so asked for a 'sandwich' as a snack. Another story suggests that he was a gambler who could not bear to leave the gaming tables, and so he needed to eat whilst continuing to play his game!

▼ *The Earl of Sandwich.*

The sandwich has become increasingly popular since that time, and has been developed to suit changing lifestyles and eating habits. Many sandwiches are quite substantial, and are sufficiently nutritious to provide a small, transportable meal. We can now buy sandwiches ready-made in plastic packages, many with exotic fillings on wholemeal and speciality breads. Of course, many sandwiches are made at home for packed lunches at school or work – they are a cheap and convenient way of providing food.

In areas of large towns or cities where there are a number of offices, shops or factories, there are often several sandwich shops, and many are thriving businesses. Often they are family-owned and run, and their products reflect the cultural mix of the local inhabitants.

Carry out a survey in your local area to find out where sandwiches are sold. You could record your findings using a database.

 ## Sandwich shops

Pret A Manger is a chain of sandwich shops and cafés, which started with one shop in 1986 and has expanded rapidly. You can find Pret A Manger shops all over London, near working areas and tourist attractions. The business is also opening shops outside the capital.

The shops sell sandwiches, salads, soups and drinks, and a variety of cakes and simple sweet dishes. The company tailors its opening hours to meet the demands of its market: the shops are open from 8 a.m. to 4 p.m., Monday to Friday. (Some shops open seven days a week for longer hours.) They open sufficiently early to catch customers who buy their lunches on their way to work. The busiest time is over lunch, but they stay open until 4 p.m. to attract tourists who may want an afternoon snack. There is no point in staying open after this time, because most people head home after work for an evening meal.

A key factor in any business is image. Pret A Manger achieve this by adopting the same stainless steel and glass interiors in every shop. This provides a modern, clean image, which is important to attract customers to this type of food retailer. This design is also practical, in that the shops are easy to clean and keep hygienic.

Each shop stocks the same range of basic items, but there are 'specials', which are new recipes or combinations produced on a regular basis. Sometimes the 'specials' will make use of seasonal produce, for example turkey and cranberry sauce sandwiches at Christmas. This addition of variety helps to maintain customer interest. The 'specials' are usually only temporary products, designed to be sold over perhaps a month-long period. However, if the new products become popular they may be developed into a permanent line. This is a good way of testing new products for their popularity.

> Look at the variety of breads and fillings used for sandwiches in two local shops or supermarkets. Record your findings.

All the shops are monitored from the Head Office, but each shop or café manager is responsible for the daily running of their branch and for the recruitment and training of their staff. Each shop has a computer terminal, which is used to order and control stock. The orders are collated, and bills are paid, by Head Office.

The company has a printed *mission statement*, which is available to be read by staff and customers in each shop. A mission statement sets out the aims and philosophy of a company, so that everyone who is employed is clear about their own role within the company, and customers are able to judge whether the staff are fulfilling the aims. The leaflet giving the mission statement includes a comments slip, which customers may complete and put into a collection box.

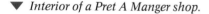

▼ *Interior of a Pret A Manger shop.*

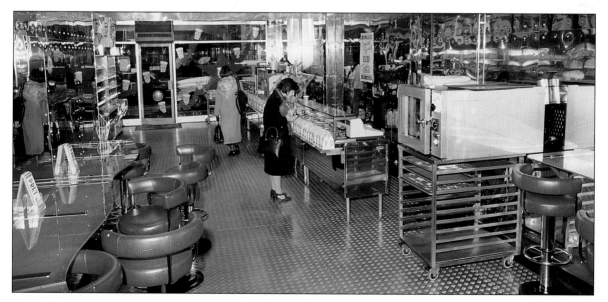

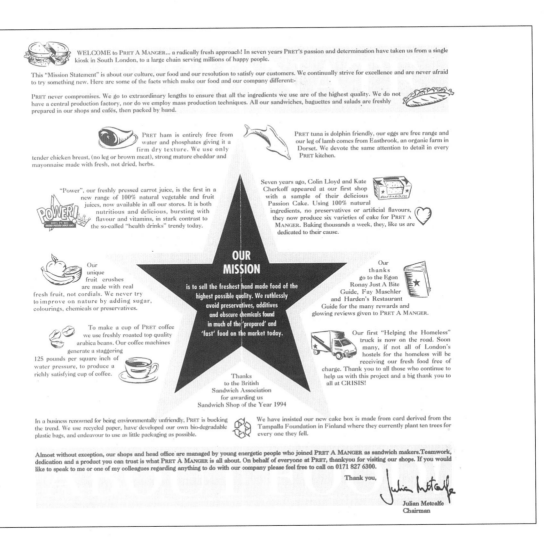

WELCOME to PRET A MANGER... a radically fresh approach! In seven years PRET'S passion and determination have taken us from a single kiosk in South London, to a large chain serving millions of happy people.

This "Mission Statement" is about our culture, our food and our resolution to satisfy our customers. We continually strive for excellence and are never afraid to try something new. Here are some of the facts which make our food and our company different:-

PRET never compromises. We go to extraordinary lengths to ensure that all the ingredients we use are of the highest quality. We do not have a central production factory, nor do we employ mass production techniques. All our sandwiches, baguettes and salads are freshly prepared in our shops and cafés, then packed by hand.

PRET ham is entirely free from water and phosphates giving it a firm dry texture. We use only tender chicken breast, (no leg or brown meat), strong mature cheddar and mayonnaise made with fresh, not dried, herbs.

PRET tuna is dolphin friendly, our eggs are free range and our leg of lamb comes from Eastbrook, an organic farm in Dorset. We devote the same attention to detail in every PRET kitchen.

"Power", our freshly pressed carrot juice, is the first in a new range of 100% natural vegetable and fruit juices, now available in all our stores. It is both nutritious and delicious, bursting with flavour and vitamins, in stark contrast to the so-called "health drinks" trendy today.

Seven years ago, Colin Lloyd and Kate Cherkoff appeared at our first shop with a sample of their delicious Passion Cake. Using 100% natural ingredients, no preservatives or artificial flavours, they now produce six varieties of cake for PRET A MANGER. Baking thousands a week, they, like us are dedicated to their cause.

Our unique fruit crushes are made with real fresh fruit, not cordials. We never try to improve on nature by adding sugar, colourings, chemicals or preservatives.

OUR MISSION

is to sell the freshest hand made food of the highest possible quality. We ruthlessly avoid preservatives, additives and obscure chemicals found in much of the 'prepared' and 'fast' food on the market today.

Our thanks go to the Egon Ronay Just A Bite Guide, Fay Maschler and Harden's Restaurant Guide for the many rewards and glowing reviews given to PRET A MANGER.

To make a cup of PRET coffee we use freshly roasted top quality arabica beans. Our coffee machines generate a staggering 125 pounds per square inch of water pressure, to produce a richly satisfying cup of coffee.

Thanks to the British Sandwich Association for awarding us Sandwich Shop of the Year 1994

Our first "Helping the Homeless" truck is now on the road. Soon many, if not all of London's hostels for the homeless will be receiving our fresh food free of charge. Thank you to all those who continue to help us with this project and a big thank you to all at CRISIS!

In a business renowned for being environmentally unfriendly, PRET is bucking the trend. We use recycled paper, have developed our own bio-degradable plastic bags, and endeavour to use as little packaging as possible.

We have insisted our new cake box is made from card derived from the Tampalla Foundation in Finland where they currently plant ten trees for every one they fell.

Almost without exception, our shops and head office are managed by young energetic people who joined PRET A MANGER as sandwich makers. Teamwork, dedication and a product you can trust is what PRET A MANGER is all about. On behalf of everyone at PRET, thankyou for visiting our shops. If you would like to speak to me or one of my colleagues regarding anything to do with our company please feel free to call on 0171 827 6300.

Thank you,

Julian Metcalfe
Julian Metcalfe
Chairman

Service in the shops has to be fast and efficient, because customers do not want to spend half their lunch hour queuing for their sandwich. There are several seats in the shops for those people who prefer to eat in, but most customers buy food to take away. The cafés have much larger seating areas and most customers 'eat in'.

Sandwiches are not cooked at the point of eating, of course, and for this reason they are a 'high-risk' food and must be stored, displayed and sold in clean, safe surroundings. 'High-risk' foods are those that are more likely to contain higher levels of bacteria, and are not necessarily cooked before being eaten. Examples include cooked meats, shellfish, dairy produce, soups and sauces.

Langers (refrigerated display cabinets) are used to store 'high-risk' products at a temperature of below 5 °C. Some of the cakes and pastries can be stored at ambient (room) temperature. The cleanliness and hygiene of each shop is vital to the success of the business – publicity resulting from a case of food poisoning could be disastrous. Floors, walls and counters must always be spotlessly clean and every member of staff who handles food has a clean set of work clothes each day.

> List ten important points to look for when deciding where to buy a sandwich or other fast food.

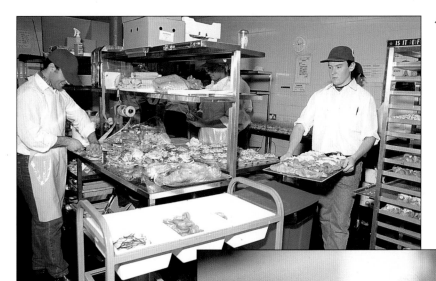

Clean conditions in a shop.

A typical lunchtime meal ▶
bought in the shop.

The City of London branch

Pret A Manger at 28 Fleet Street is a busy branch situated almost opposite the Central Law Courts in the City of London, and it is close to an area with many banks and offices. Consequently, the branch is very busy at lunchtime. An average customer spends £3–4 on their lunch. On a busy day the shop may take £3000.

The costs of producing the sandwiches vary and depend mainly on the cost of the ingredients. A large company like Pret A Manger arranges contracts with suppliers, and can buy ingredients in bulk much cheaper than you can at your local supermarket.

Make and wrap a sandwich that uses two slices of wholemeal or granary bread with a simple filling, like egg and cress or tuna and cucumber. Cost (a) the ingredients, (b) the wrapping and (c) the time taken to make the sandwich. (Assume that you will have to pay a worker at what you estimate to be a reasonable wage rate.) Work out how much you will have to charge for the sandwich to make a profit.

Extension: estimate the cost of running a shop in which to sell your sandwiches (for example, what electricity costs might be involved?). Calculate the **fixed costs** and **variable costs** for this production.

The workforce

Each shop is run by three managers, who fit into the company structure as shown in the diagram.

▼ *Management structure.*

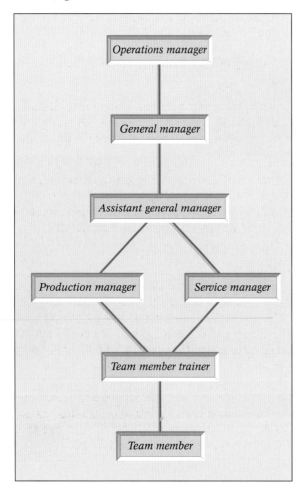

The General Manager has overall responsibility for the shop, including the organisation of work rotas, profitability, management of staff and **quality control**. The other managers are directly responsible to the General Manager. The General Manager also helps with production and service when the shop is very busy or when there is a shortage of staff.

The Production Manager is responsible for the kitchen, the production and quality of the food that is made on the premises, and all employees when they are in the kitchen. The Production Manager monitors the sales each day, and estimates the requirements for the next day's production. This is a skilled job and is almost impossible to get exactly right: the shop must not run out of any particular product (this might disappoint customers), but any food that is not sold is wasted – it cannot be kept for the next day. When the level of production for the next day has been decided, the amounts of ingredients are calculated on a computer and then ordered by telephone from the supplier. These ingredients will be delivered during the night, ready for production, which starts at 7 a.m. Each supplier has access to the shop, and goods are put into refrigerators to prevent spoilage.

The Production Manager will also ensure that sandwiches are made according to the specification set out in the manual and on time. Organising a kitchen so that production is carried out to a very high standard, as quickly and efficiently as possible, is a job that carries a great deal of responsibility. The reputation of the business rests on the quality of the products and the service.

The Service Manager deals with the management of the shop, the money taken and the training of staff for their work in the shop. She or he is also responsible for ensuring that the food in the shop is kept stocked by the relevant member of staff. It is the Service Manager's responsibility to encourage good customer relations. For example, customers are only in the shop for a short time, so it is important that staff create a good impression quickly and deal with any complaints or problems efficiently.

Set up a role-play that depicts a customer making a complaint to a member of staff. Rehearse the scene and perform it to the rest of your group. Work out a method for assessing how well the member of staff handled the situation, so that the group can evaluate the effectiveness of the customer relations within each team.

Team work

Being part of a team is an important factor in the organisation of Pret A Manger. All workers are part of a team that works together to prepare, display and sell their products, to attract new customers and to retain regular customers. Those who work in each shop are called Team Members. They are trained by the company and have a clearly laid-out job description. The company has a staff appraisal scheme. Each Team Member has an appraisal with their manager every three months. This provides an opportunity for the individual to assess their own strengths and to determine areas where more training is required. It also provides a time for discussion about future career developments.

> Organise yourselves into teams of three or four. Within your teams, decide how you would set up a mini-business. Discuss your product range, size of workforce, premises required and anything else you can think of that would be relevant. You will need to consider:
> - the type and range of products you will make,
> - what the selling price will be,
> - how many people will be involved in ordering, making and managing,
> - the detailed specification of each product,
> - the system of production for each product.

 ## *Sandwich making*

Each morning at Pret A Manger, the managers arrive at 6.30 a.m. They check the goods that have been delivered to the shop overnight, and prepare the kitchen and the shop for the arrival of the Team Members at 7.00 a.m.

The day is divided into three blocks:

- Production
  From 7.00 a.m. to 8.00 a.m. involving all staff, and from 8.00 a.m. to 11.30 a.m. involving most staff whilst one or two serve in the shop.

- Service
  From 8.00 a.m. involving one or two staff, and from 11.30 a.m. to 2.30 p.m. involving most staff whilst one or two Team Members work in the kitchen to make fresh supplies of popular lines.

- Cleaning
  From 2.30 p.m. to 4.00 p.m. for all staff except those still serving in the shop (usually two Team Members). When the shop has been closed and the cleaning has been completed to the satisfaction of the managers, the staff can go home.

Shop staff work about 45 hours each week. (In the cafés, which are open longer than the shops, a **shift** system operates.) All staff are trained to follow the six key points of production.

Draw out a chart like the one shown here to allocate jobs to staff in a busy sandwich shop. You could complete this one or design your own using your IT skills. A spreadsheet is ideal for this.

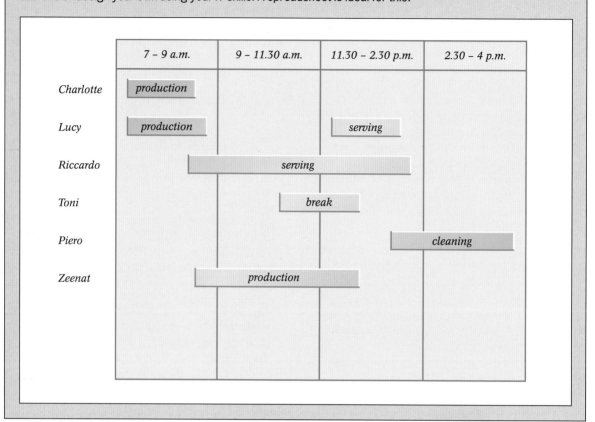

	7 – 9 a.m.	9 – 11.30 a.m.	11.30 – 2.30 p.m.	2.30 – 4 p.m.
Charlotte	production			
Lucy	production		serving	
Riccardo		serving		
Toni		break		
Piero				cleaning
Zeenat		production		

Six key points of production.

1 Use perfect ingredients

All ingredients must be of the very best quality. Never accept poor-quality ingredients – return them if necessary. Level scoops of the correct size must be used for sandwich and croissant fillings. Ingredients must be precisely weighed before use and cleaned if necessary. All slices must be the correct weight.

2 Make the product 'picture-perfect'

All recipes must be followed every time. The correct types and quantities of filling must be used for all sandwiches, salads, croissants and so on. The Production Manager must check everything that is made, by referring to the pictures of the finished products in the recipe manual. All the recipe cards must be kept clean and readable at all times. All the cooking times for baguettes, croissants and Danish pastries must be followed.

3 Be passionate about perfection

To ensure repeat business, make sure everything that is made is absolutely perfect. Every effort should be directed towards 'attention to detail'. For example, sauces on the sandwiches must be spread completely to the edges; lettuce must be broken into bite-size pieces with no discolouration; fillings should extend to the edges of the bread, so they can be seen; bread crusts must not be touching; pastries must be iced correctly. Most important of all, you must be passionate about the finished product and have pride in what you make.

4 Use the correct wrapping to keep your work fresh

Ensure that no more than five sandwiches are filled or wrapped at the same time, to keep the products as fresh as possible. Cut granary bread on the diagonal, as straight as possible. Cut Mediterranean and walnut breads completely through on the sandwich card, wrap them securely in cellophane and fasten the wrapping with one sticker in the middle of the underside. Box sandwiches carefully so that no filling touches the lid; wrap baguettes tightly in white squares of paper, wax side inwards, and secure the paper with one sticker.

5 Look after food correctly

To achieve excellent standards of hygiene, never leave or store any food items in contact with the floor – deliveries should be dated and put away in the appropriate places. Return all refrigerated items to the correct place in the fridge as soon as they have been used.

Ideally, all prepared food must be sent straight to the shop; if this is not possible then cover the food and place it in the fridge until it is needed.

6 Maintain a good rate of production

A full selection of products should be ready for the customers when the shop opens, every morning. This is achieved by a prompt start, good preparation, methodical working practices, cleaning as you go, a sense of urgency and team work.

Never sacrifice perfection for speed.

Now that you have read a little about the working philosophy of the company, write a description of the meaning of the six key points of production. Explain how you could apply them to the manufacture of other food products.

 ## *Safety*

The workplace can be dangerous, and employers must ensure that employees follow safe working codes, practices and procedures as set out in the Health and Safety at Work Act (HASAWA) 1974. This Act also covers members of the public who come into contact with the workplace. It places responsibility on both the employer and the employee for health and safety issues. The employer must ensure that the workplace is safe, by providing fire-fighting equipment, fire doors and emergency procedure notices. All this equipment must also be maintained to guarantee safety. The employees must take reasonable care of their own safety and that of other people in the workplace. They must also co-operate with the employer at all times on health and safety matters. All employers with more than four employees must provide a written statement of their health and safety policy.

List six points that you think are vital for the health and safety of the Team Members at Pret A Manger, when they are working in the kitchen.

Ingredients are all fresh – most of them are delivered daily, and many of these are ready-cooked or prepared. Others need some preparation, for example poached salmon is cooked from fresh in the shop each day. Pret A Manger use ingredients of a high quality that are free from additives and preservatives when possible. For example, the ham has no added water or phosphates, the tuna is 'dolphin-friendly', the eggs are free-range and any meat is produced on organic farms. Cakes are produced for them with 100% natural ingredients – there are no preservatives or artificial flavours. Pret A Manger also try to keep packaging to a minimum, and use recycled paper and card for their bags and boxes. Sandwiches need to be wrapped in transparent plastic so that customers can see the filling, but the company aims to use plastic as little as possible. However, although plastic packaging is often seen as an environmental problem, the evidence suggests that this is not always the case; there is more about this in the case study of Cryovac (see pages 47–49).

 ## *Hygiene*

When producing food products, workers and the preparation area must be spotlessly clean. Food handlers have a legal responsibility to customers under the 1990 Food Safety Act. Hygiene rules must be rigorously followed, to minimise the levels and growth of harmful bacteria in the food. The most common harmful bacteria found in food are shown in the table. Salmonella bacteria account for about 90% of the reported cases of food poisoning.

Bacterium	Where found
Salmonella	raw meat, poultry and eggs
Clostridium	raw meat, soil (therefore present on salads), excreta, insects
Staphylococcus aureus	in and around the human nose, mouth, throat, hair and skin

Contact your local Environmental Health Officer (you can find the address from the telephone directory or by asking at the local council offices). Ask for information about the work they do in relation to food production and kitchen premises. The Officer might be willing to come and talk to your group.

Bacteria need four things to grow and multiply:

- food,
- moisture,
- warmth,
- time.

When we prepare food, we provide food and moisture with the ingredients. We can limit the effects of warmth by storing food at a temperature either below 5 °C or above 63 °C (bacteria multiply rapidly between these temperatures, and may double in number every 10 minutes). We can account for time by ensuring that we use all food in advance of the **'Best Before' date**.

▼ *Bacteria and the correct storage temperatures for food.*

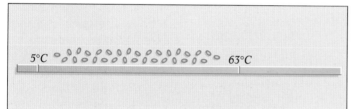

The following activity illustrates the dangers when bacteria are allowed to multiply because food is stored incorrectly.

Imagine that there are one hundred bacteria in a sandwich made at 8.00 a.m. Each bacterium divides into two every half an hour at room temperature.
- How many bacteria will there be in this sandwich if it is bought at 12.30 p.m?
- How many bacteria will there be if this sandwich is not eaten until 5.00 p.m?

Plot a graph to display your answers. You could record your data in a table like this.

Time	Number of bacteria in sandwich
8.00 a.m.	100
8.30 a.m.	200
9.00 a.m.	400
9.30 a.m.	800

List eight sources of food poisoning and ten ways in which the food handler can help prevent food poisoning from all these sources.

Hazard Analysis and Critical Control Points

Hazard Analysis and Critical Control Points (HACCPs) are very important in the manufacture of food products. They are points, particular to each product, that are identified by the Development or Production Manager as being important in the safe and consistent production of that food. For example, when producing food that is cooked but must then be chilled, it is vital that the temperature is reduced rapidly to below 5 °C. This minimises bacterial growth. Sandwich producers must identify HACCPs, mainly because most of the production is carried out at room temperature, which is ideal for bacterial growth. Identification of HACCPs is vital even when making food products which are not considered to be 'high-risk'. For example, bread or biscuits must be baked at the correct temperature and for the correct length of time to achieve the right appearance, taste and texture. For these products, the HACCPs will concern oven temperatures and cooking times.

Produce a flow-block diagram showing the procedure for making an egg and cress sandwich. Identify the HACCPs; these occur where there might be health or hygiene problems, or where a process in the manufacture must be particularly closely controlled.

Identify the HACCPs in the production of a poached salmon and watercress sandwich. Write instructions for making this sandwich in bulk, in the form of a flow chart with highlighted HACCPs.

Service

Once the main production period of the day at Pret A Manger is complete, most staff work in the shop to cope with the lunchtime period. This is when the shop does most of its business.

Good service is vital to the success of any company, and all Pret A Manger Team Members are trained to work in the shop as well as to prepare the food. The shop must be clean, efficient and welcoming, with a full range of products available throughout the day. Customers should be able to choose their food and pay with a minimum of delay. Staff ensure that hot foods are produced regularly and are still hot when they reach the customer. For example, croissants are cooked in an oven on the premises in small batches, because they can go hard if stored for long periods. They are always stored at a temperature that restricts the growth of bacteria.

Sandwiches are not individually labelled, so staff have to be able to recognise each product. Most of the shops have small seating areas, so when staff serve customers they must ask whether the food will be eaten in the shop or taken away, because the tax on take-away food is different to that on 'eat-in' food.

Customers must always be attended to courteously and promptly and thanked – the company relies on them returning for another visit.

You should now understand:

- how products are designed to meet specific needs and markets,
- materials used in food products – how they can be combined, processed and finished,
- quality control applied to the manufacture of sandwiches,
- health and safety of food products during production.

You will now be able to complete the task below, which may form part or all of your coursework.

Prepare a selection of food products to be sold either to your fellow students in school or to the public. Plan the production, packaging and distribution. Price the items by working out the cost of the ingredients. (You could use a spreadsheet to help with this.) Investigate bulk-buying from a 'Cash and Carry' store. Try out recipes and test them on a small market before making your products in bulk. Remember to consider the use of ingredients that are only available at the time of year in which you are working. For example, fresh local strawberries are only available in July.

You could use your spreadsheet to model the effect of changing the cost of ingredients. You can then look at the effect of this on the **break-even point**.

Extension: prepare a simple Business Plan for going into business on a more permanent basis. You could ask the Business Manager from a local bank or your Business Studies teacher to help you with this activity.

Packaging of food

Companies use food packaging to preserve, protect, inform and promote. A variety of materials are used in packaging, although most products have some packaging that is made from plastic. Many people are concerned about the materials used to package the products we buy in the shops, particularly plastic, because of the effect on the environment of the manufacture and disposal of packaging.

> **More about ...** the composition of packaging materials pages 46–49.

Plastic materials are used for packaging most of the fresh food that comes ready-packed, and for wrapping the food we buy at meat, fish and delicatessen counters and shops. They are also used to package foods on their journeys from the producer to the wholesale and retail outlets.

Sometimes the food is kept in the same packaging for the whole journey from the producer to the purchaser. For example, a chicken or turkey that is processed, packed and frozen by the producer and then delivered to the shop or supermarket, is sold in its original packaging. However, many foods are packaged in different ways at the different stages of the journey from producer to consumer. For example, certain types of meat may be packaged as large joints and delivered to a central wholesaler (or a central

processing plant for a supermarket chain). They will then butcher the meat and wrap it in different packaging materials for distribution to shops or supermarket shelves.

Meat may be processed or frozen and packaged at source some time before it is purchased, cooked and eaten. Developments in technology mean that bacon can now be cured in the bag. This provides a better flavour and reduces the need for the addition of a large amount of salt solution. It also gives a longer **shelf-life**. Cheeses can be similarly matured inside their vacuum packaging.

> Find out how many times a 10 kg piece of ham or a 10 kg block of Cheddar cheese may be handled from production to the end of its 'life' if it was sold **a** prepacked and **b** from the delicatessen counter. List the people who would handle the product and the processes it might go through.

Delicatessen counter. ▶

▲ *Packaged fish.*

Food which is packaged by the producer needs to look good and Vacuum Skin Packaging is one new method designed to show delicate products such as sliced cooked meats and fish at their best whilst protecting them.

Producers usually wrap foods in a heavy-duty material to withstand transportation and rough handling. This is especially true for meat, as the bones can puncture plastic that is too thin, allowing the food to become contaminated. Retailers may use the same materials, but often the packaging can be thinner and less resilient. In particular, thin, transparent plastic is used to display the food in an attractive and hygienic way. We shall now look at the four functions of packaging in more detail.

To preserve

Packaging must preserve the food not only when it is transported from the producer to the consumer, but also throughout storage at home until it is prepared and eaten. Special plastics can prolong the shelf-life of perishable foods, such as meat, cheese, cooked meats and poultry, by creating a barrier to oxygen after the product is packed under vacuum. Air is removed from inside the package at the time of sealing, and this prevents decay because bacteria need air to multiply. The plastics are resistant to the fats in the food and so the packaging does not deteriorate. At the same time foods must also be stored at the correct temperatures – see page 35. For some foods, the shelf-life is extended by adding a mixture of harmless and relatively inert gases to the package, so that the food stays fresh longer (oxygen is excluded, preventing bacteria from multiplying). This is called Modified Atmosphere Packaging (MAP). The gases used are usually carbon dioxide and nitrogen.

Some other foods, for example freshly baked bread and salad vegetables, are preserved and kept in peak condition by packing them in special plastic films, made from polypropene or polyethene, that are perforated to allow moisture to escape. This prevents the products from going soggy and rotting.

▼ *Bread products in films that allow the products to 'breathe'.*

To protect

Plastic packaging protects food from contamination by bacteria and other foreign bodies. It is vital that fresh food is protected so that it does not cause food poisoning. Customers also need to be able to examine the foods before purchase, but without contaminating them by touching, coughing or sneezing. Foods bought unpackaged, particularly meat, poultry and dairy products, are more likely to be contaminated because they are unprotected from bacteria on shelves, in the air, on people and on pests (such as flies). They are also more at risk of cross-contamination from equipment used, for example a meat slicer can transfer bacteria from one piece of meat or poultry to another. However, if proper standards of hygiene are maintained, there is no reason why unpackaged food should not be perfectly healthy. To do this, food must be displayed behind a 'sneeze barrier', which is made from glass or Perspex. Service staff must wear protective clothing and headwear, have clean hands, and use tongs and spoons to handle the food.

Packaging also protects delicate foods, and can prevent products from being damaged in transit, both from the producer to the retailer, and from the retailer to the consumer's home.

To inform

We expect to be informed about the food products we buy, so packaging displays information to assist us. The law requires that packaged food products are labelled with weight, ingredients, additives and shelf-life. Many manufacturers also include information about nutrition. A key function of packaging is to instruct us how to defrost, prepare and cook the product.

To promote

We need to be able to identify products easily. The company and brand names are usually clearly displayed, so as to attract attention. The company image can be promoted in this way, and for this reason the packaging is referred to as the 'silent salesperson'.

environmentally sound

cost effective

flexible

durable and practically unbreakable

plastic packaging

hygienic and safe

light

transparent

▲ *Advantages of plastic packaging.*

Find examples of packaging and explain how they:
- preserve,
- protect,
- inform,
- promote.

Comment on how successfully each example fulfils these functions.

Choose one or two which you think could be improved and draw up a specification for your new packaging.

Remember that it must preserve, protect, inform and promote.

Choose one food product and decide what features you would look for in the packaging for that product. Collect some samples and decide whether they fulfil the criteria that you have identified. Are there any features that you had not expected? What functions might they serve?

Development

Since the early 1960s, the price of food has generally been kept down by improving the efficiency of production and distribution. This has partly been made possible by the development of more sophisticated and cheaper forms of packaging. Food that is preserved and protected by effective packaging can be distributed over long distances without decaying or becoming contaminated. This helps prevent food being wasted. (In developing countries, up to 50% of food produced is wasted because the packaging, refrigeration and distribution systems are relatively unsophisticated.)

Also since the 1960s, we have tended to shop less frequently. Eating habits have also changed: microwave meals, pre-prepared meals and fast food are increasingly being used, and regular mealtimes are being replaced by **snacking** or **'grazing'**. The developments in the packaging of food have both prompted and enabled these changes.

Think about the implications, good and bad, for a family as a result of changing eating habits. You might interview people of different ages to examine their eating patterns. Report your findings to the rest of your group.

Up until the 1960s, there were very few foods that could be transported long distances without decaying. Since then, advances in packaging, refrigeration and transportation methods have led to us being able to enjoy fresh foods from all over the world. For example, vegetables grown in Africa can be packaged (in a film that allows the products to 'breathe'), cooled and transported by air. The shopping basket of the mid-1990s has little in common with that of the early 1960s.

Design a meal using only those foods that would have been available in the 1950s. Plan and make the meal and analyse the nutritional content. Compare it with a meal you might prepare today, looking at its content, appeal and nutritional value.

▼ *Selection of 1950s foods.*

Selection of 1990s foods. ▶

What packaging was available in the 1950s and 1960s, and how was food transported from producer to consumer?
Here is some packaging from the 1950s. How did it protect the products?

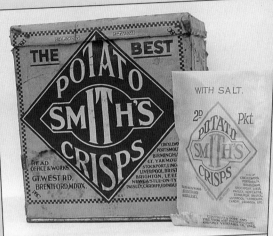

Survey your local supermarket to find the products that come from other countries. It is probably best to stick to one section of the store for your study, for example cheeses and other dairy products. Examine the types of packaging used and how the choice of packaging has influenced the availability of the products.

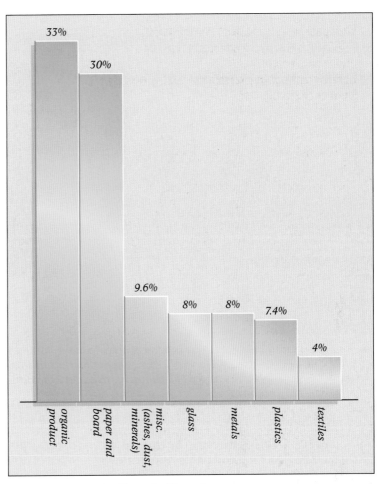

▲ Household waste.

Environmental issues

Plastic packaging is often criticised by environmental groups for encouraging a 'throw-away' lifestyle, but it is people who have created this situation. Now many plastics can be effectively recycled or re-used. Recycling the waste generated during the manufacture of packaging (for example, trimmings from the production of shopping bags) is now possible and is encouraged within the plastics industry. At the same time, consumers are being encouraged to re-use bags and containers, or dispose of them with greater care. In some countries, people are encouraged to remove excess packaging in the supermarket and leave it to be recycled. For example, in Austria recycling is actively encouraged and over-packaging is strongly discouraged. For instance, toothpaste is sold in tubes but without boxes. However, before we condemn plastics as being environmentally unfriendly, we should examine the evidence available.

The household waste we generate is mainly organic material, which consists mostly of food scraps. Only approximately 7% of the weight of household waste consists of plastic packaging.

Plastics can be effectively recycled and there are a number of schemes in operation to encourage this. The plastic packaging industry is introducing an identification and labelling system to simplify the process of sorting the different types of plastics, to make recycling cheaper and more effective. In Europe, approximately 7% of the plastic waste produced by both factories and homes is recycled.

Although plastics used for food packaging are not biodegradable this should not be seen as a disadvantage. Degradability is a slow process and the energy resources in plastic waste are not recovered. It is better to recycle the plastic, or to recover the energy through systems that burn waste to generate power for communities. Switzerland burns, under strict control, 72% of its solid waste for energy, and in Denmark 60% of waste is disposed of in this way.

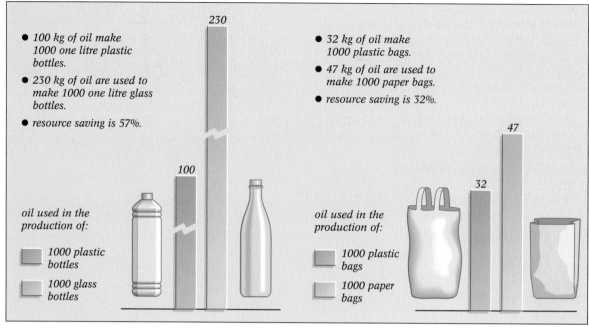

- 100 kg of oil make 1000 one litre plastic bottles.
- 230 kg of oil are used to make 1000 one litre glass bottles.
- resource saving is 57%.

- 32 kg of oil make 1000 plastic bags.
- 47 kg of oil are used to make 1000 paper bags.
- resource saving is 32%.

oil used in the production of:

▮ 1000 plastic bottles
▯ 1000 glass bottles

oil used in the production of:

▮ 1000 plastic bags
▯ 1000 paper bags

▲ Resources saved by using plastic instead of glass to make bottles, and using plastic instead of paper to wrap food. These figures include the reclaimable energy content of plastics, as well as the energy required to process the raw materials into finished goods.

Some plastic packaging is seen to be excessive by consumers. The food companies are working to reduce the amount of material used without reducing its effectiveness. Most plastic packaging in 1995 was up to 80% lighter than in 1975, and plastics are a fraction of the weight of glass. This reduces the cost of transporting the products, especially the amount of fuel used, which reduces the consequent pollution. For example, if mineral water is delivered in plastic bottles rather than glass, there is a 39% fuel saving.

Plastics are made from oil, which is a limited resource. The production of plastics uses about 4% of the total quantity of oil used in Europe, whereas heating, transport and energy production use 86% of the total. We each use 15–20 kilograms of plastic packaging in a year, and the equivalent amount of petrol needed to make this would be enough for a 150–200 kilometre (93–125 mile) car journey. Of course we do not use the same types of oils for these

two purposes, but this example gives you an idea of how little oil (relative to the amounts used for transport) is used for the production of packaging of food.

Investigate the schemes in operation locally for recycling plastics. Are they adequate? Find out what more could be achieved, and write to your local council suggesting improved methods for recycling and recovery.

Carry out a survey of your local shops and supermarkets, for evidence that they encourage recycling. Make a list of these incentives and survey customers to find out how much they recycle regularly. Write a report for the retailers and develop a plan of action for them to improve the recycling habits of their customers.

You should now understand:
- the development of materials for food packaging,
- the qualities of materials used for food packaging,
- the design and manufacture of food packaging,
- how developments in transportation have improved the quality and availability of food products,
- the factors that affect food during transport and storage,
- the effects of the production and use of packaging materials on the environment.

You will now be able to complete the task below, which may form part or all of your coursework.

TASK

Develop a new dish that is to be sold in a supermarket or specialist food shop. Prepare the dish and photograph it. Refer to your photograph(s) to design the packaging, and state which materials you will use. Explain how your packaging could be recycled or recovered.

The composition of packaging materials

Designers of packaging need to know about the structures of materials. This knowledge helps them to select, process and finish packaging to meet specific design criteria. The methods used to process and finish the packaging are also dependent upon the structures of the materials.

The packaging of food products involves a range of compliant and resistant materials. Metals are used for many types of packaging. The other major type of packaging materials are polymers. Natural polymers, particularly wood-based materials such as card or paper, and synthetic (manufactured) polymers are used.

Metal packaging materials

Metals are used in a wide range of packaging products, ranging from aluminium alloy foils to tin-plated steel cans. Metals are a large group of elements that have certain physical and chemical properties in common, such as resistance to corrosion and conduction of heat. Most metals can be worked: they will change shape rather than break when they are placed under pressure or struck by tools and machines. Metals that can be beaten or rolled into thin sheets are said to be *malleable*, and those that can be drawn into wire-like shapes are said to be *ductile*.

Look around you at all the metal-based packaging in your kitchen at home or in school. List the type of product the packaging is used for, the metal it is made from and how you think it was made. What properties would the metal need to allow it to be used for each type of packaging?

An *alloy* is produced when a metal is combined with one or more other elements, which may be metals or non-metals. Alloys have physical properties that may differ considerably from those of the pure metal. By adjusting the proportions of the elements in the mix, alloys can be made that have great hardness, toughness, mechanical strength and resistance to corrosion. Many alloys used in tools and packaging for food are based on copper, aluminium and iron. For example, the stainless steel in many kitchen utensils is an alloy of iron, chromium, nickel and carbon.

Oxo metal storage tins. ▶

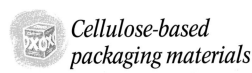

Cellulose-based packaging materials

The properties of paper and card explain their role as major packaging materials. They are easy to shape and join, and card is moderately resilient – it can resist light forces that may be applied during transportation or by the customer's handling of the product. Paper and card are also easy to print upon, so they can be used for product labelling.

> Look at the range of card and paper packaging in your kitchen at home or in school. Select one example of packaging and carefully disassemble it to find out how it was shaped, folded, joined and printed upon. Draw the net (outline shape) of the flattened-out package on a sheet of A4. (You may need to scale the drawing to fit onto the page.) Add labels that describe the key design features of the package. Produce a step-by-step set of drawings to show how the manufacturer of the package folded it from a flat shape into the three-dimensional shape with which you started.

Plastic packaging materials

Plastics are a very large group of synthetic materials with structures based on carbon atoms. An important characteristic of plastics is that when heated, they can be easily moulded. Thousands of different plastics have been manufactured since the 1940s and these have been used in a wide range of products, including furniture, vehicles and packaging materials. The physical and chemical properties of a plastic determine how it can be used. Ethene-based plastics, for example polyethene, are the simplest of the plastic materials used in packaging. Polyethene is sometimes known as polyethylene or polythene. It is a soft, flexible, waxy material produced in different grades: for example, low density polyethene (LDPE), medium density (MDPE) and high density (HDPE).

> Collect examples of plastic packaging and try to identify the type of plastic used. What do you think will happen to this type of plastic once its job has been done?

Cryovac* is the packaging division of W.R. Grace & Co. Grace Packaging is one of the world's leading innovators in flexible plastic packaging systems. Its Cryovac* films, laminates and bags preserve the freshness and extend the shelf-life of products such as meat, poultry, cheese, fish, vegetables and salads.

Cryovac* have many manufacturing centres around the world, one of which is situated in St. Neots in Cambridgeshire, UK. The factory there produces a wide range of packaging for all types of food, and about 500 people are employed there.

Cryovac* invest considerable sums of money in researching and developing combinations of plastics to make packaging. Their packaging is used by both the producers and the retailers of foods.

Packaging material often contains many layers of several types of plastic, such as polyethene, polypropene, polyesters and polyamides. This is because food manufacturers require packaging materials that are designed for their individual needs. For example, a company that makes cheese will need different packaging to a company that processes cooked ham. The vacuum packaging around these two products may look the same, but will be composed of a different combination of layers.

For these reasons Cryovac* has developed a range of shrinkable bags and multi-layered films to meet the requirements of food manufacturers.

Shrink packaging

Shrinking provides a second-skin effect.

Some plastics exhibit a property known as *plastic shrink memory*. If a piece of this kind of plastic is heated, shaped and cooled, it will return to its original size when exposed again to heat. If a film of this plastic is heated and wrapped around a food product, the film will shrink when heated to form a protective barrier. The wrapper closely fits the shape of the product, almost like a 'second skin'.

Cryovac* have developed these plastics to suit various different products. The films can be made to several thicknesses and strengths, some can let water in or out, and some films can be left on the product whilst it is cooked.

▼ *Diagram to explain plastic shrink memory.*

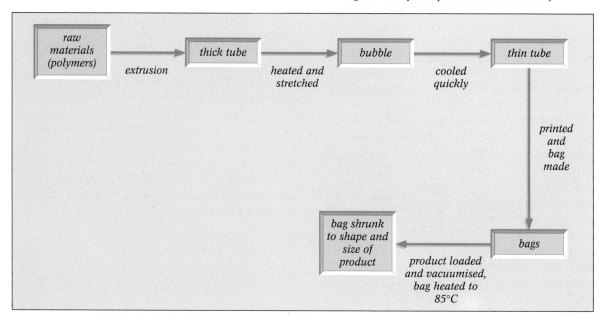

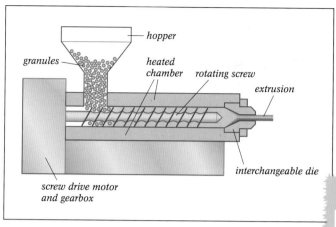

▲ *Extrusion machine.*

Cryovac* produce bags by extruding molten plastic to form a narrow tube. The extruded tube is reheated and blown with compressed air to make a wider tube with thinner walls. This tube is then printed with any labelling required, and cut into bags of different shapes and sizes. When a bag is eventually used for packaging food, it is exposed to heat (using either hot air or water), and the bag will try to shrink back to its original, narrow tube shape. The shape of the food prevents it doing so, and the bag has been shrunk around the food product.

You should now understand:

- **the types of materials used to package food,**
- **the properties of metals and plastics that make them suitable for food packaging,**
- **the use of plastic shrink memory,**
- **how different plastics are used for different layers and types of packaging.**

TASK

You will now be able to complete the task below, which may form part or all of your coursework.

Choose a food product that is familiar to you, such as an egg. Use a computer-based drawing package to design and make your own net to re-package the product in a new way. Concentrate on the structural aspects of the package (there is no need to put any labelling or graphics onto your package). Compare your package with the existing product. How can you test your package to see if it is an improvement on an existing package?

Produce a short report to explain how you set up your investigation and made sure it was a fair test.

▼ *Cryovac* multilayer bag construction for packaging cheese.*

*Cryovac is the registered trade name of W.R. Grace & Co.

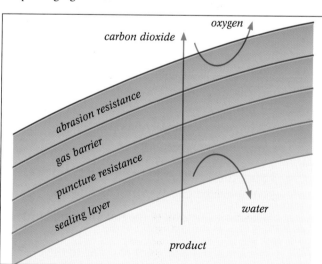

The multilayer construction keeps the water content constant within the cheese, whilst allowing carbon dioxide to escape as the cheese matures, but preventing oxygen from causing mould growth.

Appendix: Market research

Market research is the process by which information about a product or market is collected, so as to inform company decision-making. Techniques used to research products and their markets fall into four categories.

1 Primary research

This provides general information gathered directly from the public by means of surveys or questionnaires.

2 Secondary research

This provides information that can be extracted from existing published documents, market surveys, reports and computer databases.

3 Quantitative research

This research technique involves the use of a large, representative sample of people. The people selected may be interviewed or asked to fill in detailed and sometimes lengthy forms. The more people interviewed in the research, the more the results of the research can be trusted.

4 Qualitative research

This is a more focused technique. Small groups of people or individuals are consulted in order to find out about their attitudes and responses to particular products. This method provides a much more detailed set of responses to questions. Its value as a research method is limited because it relies on the subjective opinions of people. The information is more difficult to collect, and it is much harder to analyse the data. It is subjective because you will be canvassing opinions and attitudes rather than verifiable facts (objective research).

Survey and questionnaire design

With the exception of secondary research, each survey activity requires the design of a survey or questionnaire to collect and record information for future analysis.

The pieces of information that you collect are the data. The analysis of this information is known as data analysis. You need to plan your questions carefully so that you collect useful and relevant information. There are four different types of question that you might consider.

1 Closed questions provide yes/no type responses, or offer a limited choice of answer.

Have you heard about the ...? yes/no
Do you like the sound of ...?
a little / a lot / neither like nor dislike / not at all.

2 Open-ended questions are useful for finding out about attitudes or opinions, but they produce a wide variety of responses that take time to interpret and categorise.

What do you think about . . . ?
What do you like about . . . ?

3 Structured questions break a long and complicated question into manageable parts.

Describe the look of the food product. Is it:
interesting/dull
pleasing to the eye/not pleasing to the eye?

4 Rating questions use a scaling system and give a quick indication of attitudes and opinions. Answers can be coded and analysed numerically, for example '68% of people think that ...'

Which face sums up how you feel about the taste of this product?

Glossary

Batch production
Groups or batches of similar items that are produced at the same time.

'Best Before' date
The last date for eating recommended by the manufacturer.

Break-even point
The point at which all the costs involved in making a product have been paid for in sales and the company begins to make a profit.

Concept samples
Samples of a new food product made for tasting and evaluation during the development stage.

Continual flow production
Products pass through a number of stages with each stage adding to the make up of the overall product.

Fixed costs
Costs which are regular and do not change significantly when production increases, for example loans and rents.

Grazing
See **snacking**.

HACCPs (Hazard Analysis and Critical Control Points)
Points during manufacture when processes have to be carefully controlled or monitored to ensure that a product is made according to the specification and that it conforms to high standards of hygiene.

Market research
The study of the likes and dislikes of consumers.

One-off production
Every item that is produced is different. It is the most labour-intensive form of production. Usually refers to 'hand-made' products.

Own label
The label on the product is the name of the shop or supermarket chain and not that of the manufacturer.

Pilot plant
A small section of a factory which is equipped with the same facilities as the main production lines but can be adapted to trial new products before full scale production starts.

Production samples
Samples of a new product made on a development production line to check that the recipe and production on a large scale will be possible.

Quality assurance
The process of monitoring the stages of manufacture of a product to ensure that quality standards are being met.

Quality control
A system used in factories (or anywhere that products are manufactured) to check that finished products meet the required specification.

Repetitive flow production

The production of large numbers of identical products. This type of production system enables manufacturing companies to offer their products at competitive prices.

Sell-by date

The last date of sale recommended by the manufacturer.

Shelf-life

The length of time for which a food product remains edible.

Shift

A period of time worked by people, usually in a factory, when continuous production is required. Many factories operate 24 hours in three 8-hour shifts.

Shift worker

Someone who works at different times during the day, depending on the times they are allocated by a rota. The period of time worked is called a 'shift'. Shift workers are employed in businesses, often factories, that operate continuously for up to 24 hours a day.

Snacking

The habit of eating small meals or snacks at frequent and regular intervals during the day rather than eating larger meals less often. Sometimes called **grazing**.

Variable costs

Costs of materials and the production process, which increase as larger quantities of a product are manufactured.

Index